CITY OF WINCHESTER

THE ANCIENT CAPITAL OF ENGLAND

ABOVE: *One of the prettiest and least altered fronts in the High Street. The county newspaper, 'The Hampshire Chronicle', moved to these premises in 1813.* FRONT COVER: *The Priory Stables and Cheyney Court, within the 15th-century gateway to the Cathedral Close.* BACK COVER: *A general view of Winchester looking west.*

CITY OF WINCHESTER

BARBARA CARPENTER TURNER

WINCHESTER, once the capital of England, lies within a fold of the Hampshire downs and at an important crossing of the River Itchen. In recent years the city has expanded very rapidly. Within the centre of the city some old street frontages have disappeared and with them a number of interesting buildings. Yet much of the essential charm of Winchester remains and an observant visitor must carry away with him the memory of a great cathedral and a secluded close, the beauty and interest of St. Cross and of Winchester College, the presence of the river and of the mills, and of houses large and small, roofed with the hand-made tiles which help to give Winchester its characteristic colouring.

Around the city and within its western and eastern quarters are the downs. The earliest known inhabitants lived on St. Catherine's Hill, on Hockley Down, and on the western hill near the Westgate. When the Romans came, the settlement of people in the centre of the town increased in size and in importance. Its Latin name, Venta Belgarum, perhaps means the market town of the Belgii, and Winchester was one of the two capitals of their canton.

Of the Roman town itself comparatively little can be known without a complete excavation of the entire city centre. Intermittent but careful recent excavation has revealed some details of the Roman layout; a Roman main road seems to have followed almost the same line as the present High Street; Middle Brook Street continued across the High Street in a southerly direction. There were great public buildings; early in 1953 a long length of tessellated pavement in a red and white key pattern was found in St. George's Street; from the same site, a fragmentary Roman inscription perhaps relating to one of the Antonine emperors has the largest Roman lettering yet found anywhere in England. Venta Belgarum is also known to have been an important centre for the making of cloth. Parts of the walls date from the Roman era and the settlement in the centre of the city was potentially capable of expansion to include the whole walled area.

Under what circumstances the Romans left Winchester we do not know. Presumably the Romano-British inhabitants stayed on after the departure of the garrison, if there was one. Eventually there came the barbarians, perhaps the Jutes, and certainly those people conveniently

Continued on page 5

*   *   *

LEFT: *The Westgate, once one of the main gateways into the walled city, and now a museum housing a fine local collection. The view from the top is always interesting, but the appearance of the gate has not been improved by alterations for modern traffic.*

FACING PAGE: *No one knows how or when the High Cross was first set up in the city. Much of the original structure has gone, but a date of about 1450 has been suggested. Behind the Cross stands the tall building which used to be known as Heaven. To the left is Hell, perhaps so called from the flames and smoke which may have come from the Royal Mint which stood behind it.*

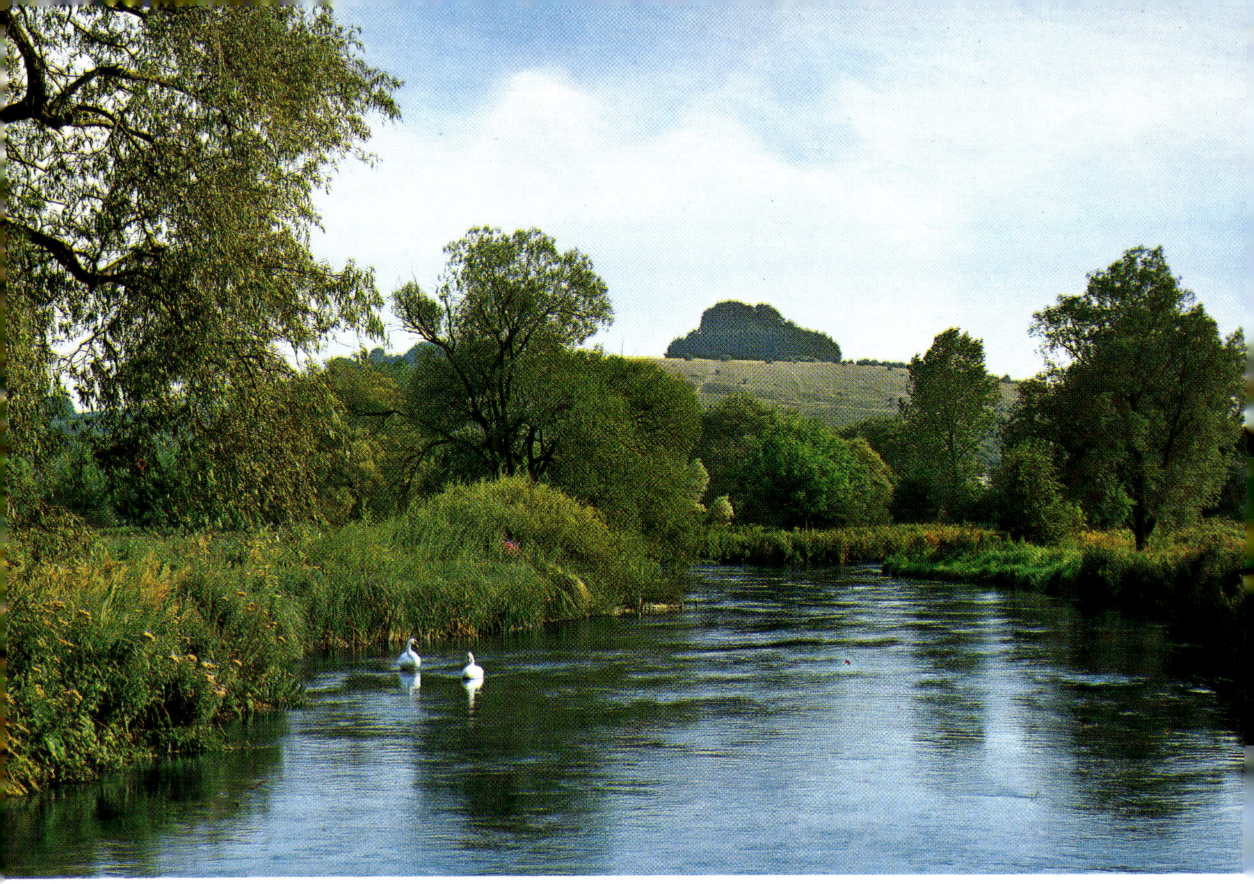

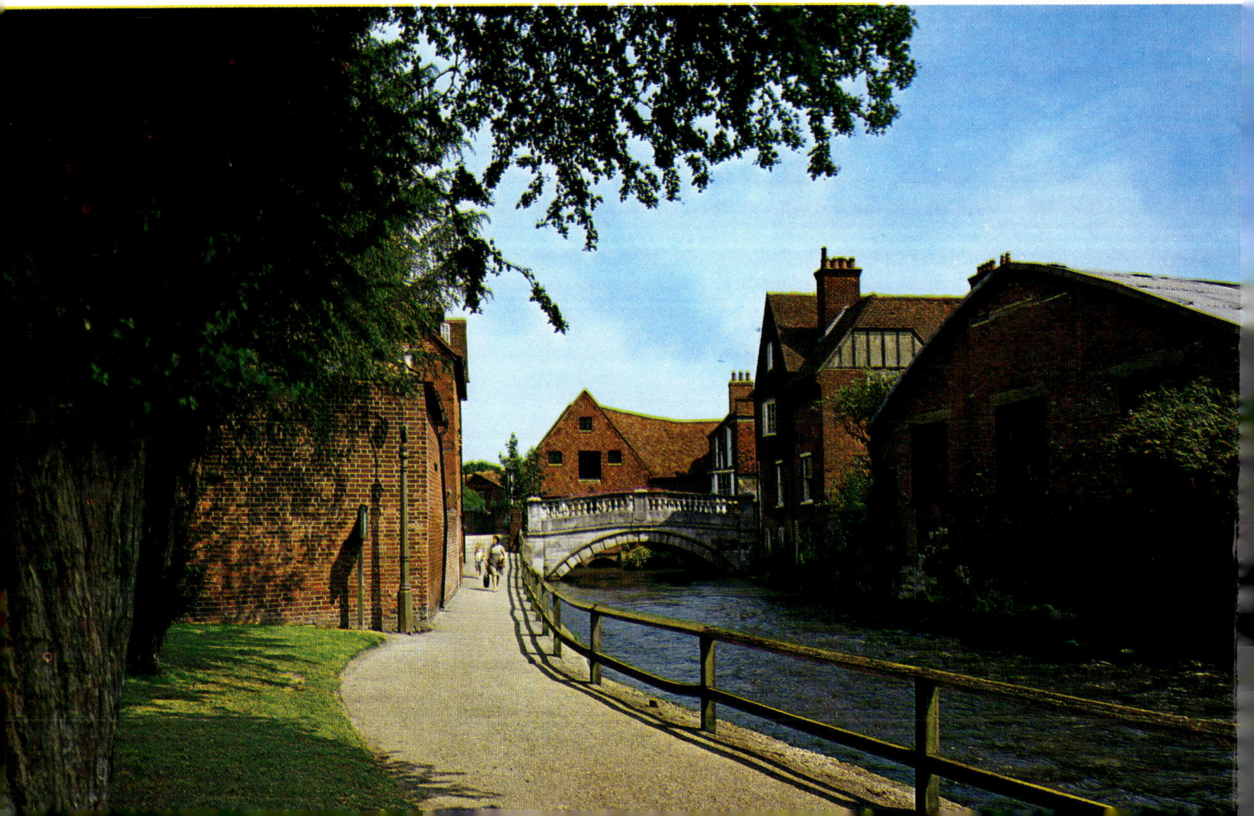

called the Anglo-Saxons. They were pagans; a very recent excavation at Winnall has disclosed a pagan Anglo-Saxon cemetery there, and some interesting grave furniture, including a fine brooch. The Anglo-Saxons may have found a small Christian community in Romano-British Winchester but their own conversion to Christianity in the early years of the seventh century A.D. meant the beginning of a new era. When Wessex became the predominant kingdom in England, Winchester became the national capital, and even after the Norman Conquest of 1066 the city continued to share this honour with London until about the middle of the twelfth century. The earliest known building within the Christian city was the first Saxon cathedral, dedicated to St. Peter and St. Paul, built by King Cenwealh after his conversion in c.645, and known as the Old Minster. There was perhaps also a royal palace in the High Street and later a house for the bishop at Wolvesey, after the bishop's chair (*cathedra*) had been moved to Winchester Cathedral from Dorchester-on-Thames, the original centre of the Winchester diocese. The ordinary inhabitants lived in cottages often little better than hovels. The stone buildings of the Roman town were either gradually covered over or perhaps used as quarries for the cathedral or for the chapels dependent on it which eventually became the parish churches.

Continued on page 6

*   *   *

FACING PAGE, above: *The River Itchen and St. Catherine's Hill form one of the most famous views of the Winchester scene. The river rises near Alresford and flows down to the sea at Southampton. The pre-Roman bank round St. Catherine's Hill can clearly be seen.*

FACING PAGE, below: *The city mill which originally belonged to the priory of Wherwell. In 1554 it was granted to the Corporation by royal charter. The present building was erected in 1743–44.*

RIGHT: *Alfred's statue in the Broadway. In 1901, the then Mayor of Winchester, Alfred Bowker, gained nationwide support for his suggestion that there ought to be a national memorial to Alfred the Great, founder of the English nation. Hamo Thornycroft's very fine statue is the result.*

Wessex was all too soon threatened by the raids and invasions of new pagan hordes, the Vikings of the north. Tradition assigns the building of a great wall round the cathedral close to St. Swithun, bishop of Winchester. It was this wall which saved the townspeople from the Danes in 860. Swithun is remembered not only as an excellent bishop but also as a worker of miracles and a man of humility, who did not wish for a magnificent tomb. Heaven's disapproval of the moving of the saint's body from its original modest resting place may be shown by rain on his day (15th July) and rain for forty days after. Alfred, who was perhaps Swithun's pupil, turned back the Danes from his kingdom and Winchester prospered. To the fine buildings already in the city he and his son, Edward, added a convent of nuns (St. Mary's, Nunnaminster), and another foundation for monks, known as Newminster to distinguish it from the old cathedral. Newminster moved to the suburb of Hyde in the reign of Henry I. In the reign of Edgar, thanks to that king and to Bishop Ethelwold of Winchester, the monastic foundations were reformed and handed over to religious of the Benedictine rule who remained in possession of

*　　　*　　　*

ABOVE: *This timber-framed house is traditionally known as the Old Rectory of St. Peter Chesil Church, which stands on the opposite side of the same road, the Street of the Chesil, or Strand of the River Itchen. The building used to be two cottages; its ground floor was cut back when it was restored in 1893 and its rails have been recently removed.*

LEFT: *The church of St. Peter Chesil viewed from The Weirs, a walk along the River Itchen. Adjoining the church, which is now a theatre, can be seen part of the fine Elizabethan house of Sir Thomas Flemyng, the famous judge.*

FACING PAGE: *St. John's in the Soke, otherwise known as St. John in Montibus or St. John Uppe-Down. There were six churches dedicated to St. John in medieval Winchester. This church in the Bishop's Soke is the most unaltered of Winchester parish churches. It has fine wall paintings, an Easter Sepulchre, the remains of a rood staircase, a number of mural memorials, and an Elizabethan clock now in the City Museum.*

their three abbeys until the dissolution of the monasteries in 1539. Ethelwold rebuilt the cathedral, giving it a famous organ and weather vane. The *scriptorium* of the monastery became a centre for manuscript writing and illumination famous all over Europe as the 'Winchester School'. To this period belongs the Benedictional of St. Ethelwold, written by a scribe of the Old Minster, but kept in Hyde Abbey. Ethelwold is also said to have improved the water courses and developed the area now known as the Brooks, a tradition borne out by recent archaeological evidence.

The traditional connection between the kings of England and the Winchester monasteries continued during the years when England was ruled by the Dane, Canute. He and his wife, Emma, gave many gifts to the great churches, and on her death in 1052, she left one of her most important Winchester properties, the Manor of Godbegot, to the cathedral. The Danish dynasty did not last long. Hardicanute was succeeded by his half-brother, Emma's son, Edward the Confessor, the last Anglo-Saxon

king of England. He was crowned in Winchester Cathedral.

The Norman Conquest brought many changes. Winchester was probably too important, like London, to be included in the Domesday Book, but it was the subject of two separate surveys made in *c*. 1110 and in 1148, bound together in a magnificent 12th-century binding and known as the *Winchester Domesday*.

The earliest survey compares the city of 1110 with the situation as it was *'Tempus Regis Edwardi'*, in the time of King Edward the Confessor, and this provides our first real glimpse of local government. The Conquest had brought about a decrease in the population and widespread demolition of the southern side of the centre of the High Street where burgesses' houses had come down to make way for a royal palace and administrative offices, royal mints and forges. A fundamental feature of Winchester's history has been the fact that much of the city was royal demesne, in which most property was held by burgess tenure. Though a small tax was payable to the king as

overlord, each burgess had the right to buy or sell or let his own property, provided the transaction was publicly recorded in open court. Since the king was overlord his interests in the city were represented by a reeve, *prepositus,* and the reeves of Winchester were the earliest officials of whose activities we have any real knowledge. Yet even the reeve dared not claim that all Winchester obeyed him. Emma's Manor of Godbegot, and the Cloth Hall (on the site of Marks & Spencer's store) acknowledged neither the reeve nor his later successor the mayor, and a very large area outside the walls but including the present southern and eastern quarters of the town acknowledged only the bishop, had its own law courts, and was known as the Soke. The Soke's jurisdiction also included a number of houses belonging to the bishop within the walls. The second survey included in the volume known as the *Winchester Domesday* was compiled as a financial record for Bishop Henry de Blois in 1148.

After the death of Henry I in 1135, civil war broke out and Winchester

was frequently desecrated by the opposing armies of the bishop, Henry de Blois, who supported his brother Stephen, and of the Empress Matilda, Henry I's daughter and heiress. It looked as if the future overlord of Winchester might well be the bishop, and not the king. Henry de Blois rebuilt Wolvesey as a great fortress palace, using some materials from the royal palace in the High Street. Much of the town was burnt, but a quick revival not only of commerce but of the royal supremacy followed in the reign of Henry II (1155–1184). The new royal castle on the western hill was rapidly developed. Bishop de Blois is gratefully remembered today as the founder of St. Cross Hospital.

This was a period of prosperity. The monasteries flourished, and Winchester became once more a great centre for the arts. The Winchester Vulgate is the best example of this twelfth-century renaissance. To this period also belong the surviving specimens of ivory carving, work in enamels, and beautiful leather bindings, all of which are unsurpassed examples of beauty and good taste.

By the middle of the twelfth century too, local government had made considerable progress, and for a brief period the city gained the right of returning its own farm to the king direct through its reeve, Stigand, and not through the sheriff of the county. Stigand perhaps helped to gain the city its earliest surviving royal charters, grants to the Gild Merchant and to the citizens, which almost certainly date from 1155. It is clear that the existence of these two separate charters, each granting rights to separate groups, implies some sort of struggle for power within the city, a struggle to decide which group should lead a movement to exclude, not the king, but his officer, the sheriff of the county. At first the Gild Merchant was successful, but eventually the city's government emerged as a council of twenty-four, led by two bailiffs and a senior official soon known as the mayor. The first mention of a mayor of Winchester occurs in 1200. The corporation met for its general business, including the election of officers, in St. John's House on the north-eastern end of the High Street. The city court which dealt with all kinds of commercial and civil offences, the enrolling of private charters relating to the transfer of burgess property, and the local legal process known as setting a stake for the recovery of property, met in the 'Hall of Court of the city', a building which was first near the High Cross and then in a large tenement which later became known as the Guildhall, on the corner of St. Thomas Street and the High Street, now the Queen Anne Guildhall.

From the reign of Henry III onwards every English sovereign confirmed by royal charter the rights of the citizens of Winchester; the mayor was acknowledged as head of the corporation, but there was no real act of incorporation until the great charter of Elizabeth I (1587).

Winchester flourished in the early Middle Ages. The city had its own seal, affixed to all official documents, and from 1337 was allowed to return its own farm to the Exchequer without the sheriff as intermediary. A tolerant religious policy allowed the Winchester Jews in their unenclosed ghetto to live peacefully with their fellow citizens. Hampshire wool from the neighbouring downs laid the foundation for many a medieval fortune. Each year merchants came from

Continued on page 10

*　　*　　*

FACING PAGE, above: *The miller's house on the College Mill Stream.*

FACING PAGE, below: *A view of St. Thomas Street, showing the old Guildhall. This site is first recorded in 1295 when it was a large block of cottages and an inn. After the Black Death it was made the Hall of Court, the second building to be called by that name.*

ABOVE: *This gateway was once an entrance to Hyde Abbey, the Benedictine monastery founded by Alfred and his son, Edward. The gate and surviving walls have been restored. The monastery went to Hyde in Henry I's reign. It was also known as Newminster to distinguish it from the other Benedictine community which served the Cathedral.*

RIGHT: *Avebury House is an 18th-century residence with a good Doric doorway and much panelling inside. The worked stones in the southern wing may have come from the demolished church of St. Swithun nearby. From 1820 to 1937 the house was owned by the Mayo family. Charles Mayo was Chief Surgeon of the County Hospital for 50 years and mayor three times. His son specialised in battlefield surgery in the American Civil War. The family were also rectors of Avebury, Wilts., for five generations.*

all over Europe to attend the bishop's fair held on St. Giles' Hill. Another source of local prosperity were the many mills, some of them grinding mills. Segrim's on Wharf Hill, Durngate, and St. Cross are surviving examples which belonged to the bishop. The fulling mills on the main river at Coitbury were given to the city by King John to be held by the corporation. A feature of the medieval layout which has survived in a few places is the narrow lane leading out of the High Street and forming an entrance to the wider side street proper.

In 1290 the Jews were expelled from England. The area of the Winchester ghetto seems to have remained undeveloped for many years. A second and much more serious setback occurred in 1348–51 with the dreadful Black Death. At least half the population died. Churches, houses, whole streets were desolate and

ruined. Many of the smaller parish churches disappeared for ever, and population was concentrated into an area 'within the precincts of the High Street'. The rebuilding of much of the cathedral by two successive bishops, Edington (1344–1366) and Wykeham (1366–1404), stands as a great act of faith offered in a desolate diocese. The High Cross was perhaps set up at this time, as a thank-offering, though it may be slightly earlier.

Another sign of revival and prosperity was the foundation of Winchester College by Bishop William of Wykeham. Those citizens with money to spare found speculation in real estate highly profitable. Amongst them was Mark le Faire, mayor five times between 1398 and 1415, who rebuilt a large part of the ghetto as the George Inn on the north eastern junction of the High Street and Jewry Street. Eventually all the le Faire property passed to the corporation

who were empowered in 1442 by royal charter to acquire land to increase their revenues. From the fifteenth century onwards, however, the corporation never considered it had money sufficient for its needs; the later charters grant temporary financial relief rather than important new constitutional privileges.

With the accession of the first Tudor king, Henry VII, in 1485, it seemed as if Winchester might once more become the royal capital. The king was anxious to establish his family as one of ancient lineage. His eldest son, Arthur, was christened in Winchester Cathedral. His second son and successor, Henry VIII, was proud to show a visiting Hapsburg (the Emperor Charles V) King Arthur's Round Table in the Castle hall in 1522. Yet Henry VIII's religious policy brought about a great change in Winchester. With the dissolution of the monasteries in 1538 and 1539, large areas of Winchester were desolate. Hyde Abbey and St. Mary's were both pulled down, and the sites used as stone quarries. Neither were redeveloped till the eighteenth century; in St. Mary's precinct the Recorder of Winchester, William Pescod, built himself a fine residence just before 1751, now known as Abbey House. At Hyde, a county bridewell was erected, on the site of the monastery, to the disgust of many distinguished antiquarians who felt that it was an act of sacrilege thus to scatter the

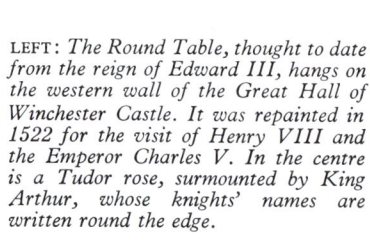

*   *   *

LEFT: *The Round Table, thought to date from the reign of Edward III, hangs on the western wall of the Great Hall of Winchester Castle. It was repainted in 1522 for the visit of Henry VIII and the Emperor Charles V. In the centre is a Tudor rose, surmounted by King Arthur, whose knights' names are written round the edge.*

FACING PAGE, left: *This Wren-style house at No. 4 St. Peter Street, of which the northern wing has been pulled down, was apparently built for the Duchess of Portsmouth, mistress of Charles II, in the late 17th century.*

FACING PAGE, right: *The Eclipse Inn, so called in opposition to the nearby Sun, now a dress shop. The front is a modern restoration of a building which was once the rectory of the church of St. Lawrence.*

bones of England's Alfred. This bridewell was closed in 1850.

Of the great monasteries, therefore, only St. Swithun's survived as a new foundation of Dean and Chapter, but the fabric of the cathedral was much altered by the religious changes. St. Swithun's Shrine was demolished in 1539, at dead of night, and in the presence of the mayor, Richard Bethell, an ardent reformer who bought the site of Hyde Abbey as a financial speculation. In the reign of Edward VI extremists among the local Protestants disfigured the High Cross. It was restored by William Laurens, mayor in 1554, on the occasion of the marriage of Philip and Mary in Winchester Cathedral. So heavy was civic expenditure on this occasion that the city was granted a series of Royal Letters Patent giving it various forms of financial compensation. A particularly welcome grant was that of the Winchester properties of Wherwell Abbey, Southwick Priory and St.

Mary's Abbey with its Charnel Chapel. The corporation thus acquired yet another important addition to its real estate, and continued to hold all its properties till the beginning of the nineteenth century. In 1587–8 the city obtained a new charter setting out the constitution as it had emerged from the Middle Ages. The negotiations were carried out by Sir Francis Walsingham, who had married into a Southampton family, and had graciously consented to become the city's first High Steward.

The castle was now more of a royal liability than an asset but still sufficiently strong, however, to be the chief centre of Royalist resistance when Winchester was besieged by Parliamentarian troops in the Civil War. If a broad view of Winchester's history be taken it is interesting to notice the spirit of compromise with which both corporation and citizens met the great crises of our national history. In the reign of Charles I it is not surprising

that the citizens hesitated at first to declare themselves either for King or Parliament. In 1642 they returned one Royalist, Sir William Ogle, to the House of Commons and one Parliamentarian, the notorious regicide lawyer John Lisle, who was already Recorder of Winchester. The taking of the city by Cromwell in 1645, however, stiffened Royalist feeling, and when Charles I came to the Westgate in 1648, as a prisoner, he was given the loyal reception traditionally given to monarchs. The mayor and corporation met him and surrendered the mace. The corporation had retained this ancient emblem of its delegated authority, though it had previously handed over some of its plate, chiefly cups and bowls, to be melted down for the Royalist army.

The western castle was eventually dismantled. The great hall, with the Round Table, passed into the hands of the county authorities, and was used as one of the Assize Courts

Continued on page 14

ABOVE: *View of the south side of the Cathedral, and the Close and the Deanery. The vast length of the Cathedral roof is apparent, and the varying architectural styles of the Deanery, formerly the Prior's Lodging. The roofs of the Deanery buildings are one of Winchester's great features, including Frampton's Long Gallery of c. 1662.*

LEFT: *The effigy of William of Wykeham, founder of Winchester College, and greatest of all the Bishops of Winchester. On 27th September each year the Cathedral observes his obit, the day of his death. The figures at his feet are probably his secretaries.*

FACING PAGE: *The High Altar and reredos. The original altar screen was probably 15th-century, but it was ruthlessly defaced at the Reformation, although the carving of the canopy, of superb workmanship, survived. The carpet in front of the High Altar was used at Westminster for the Coronation of George VI.*

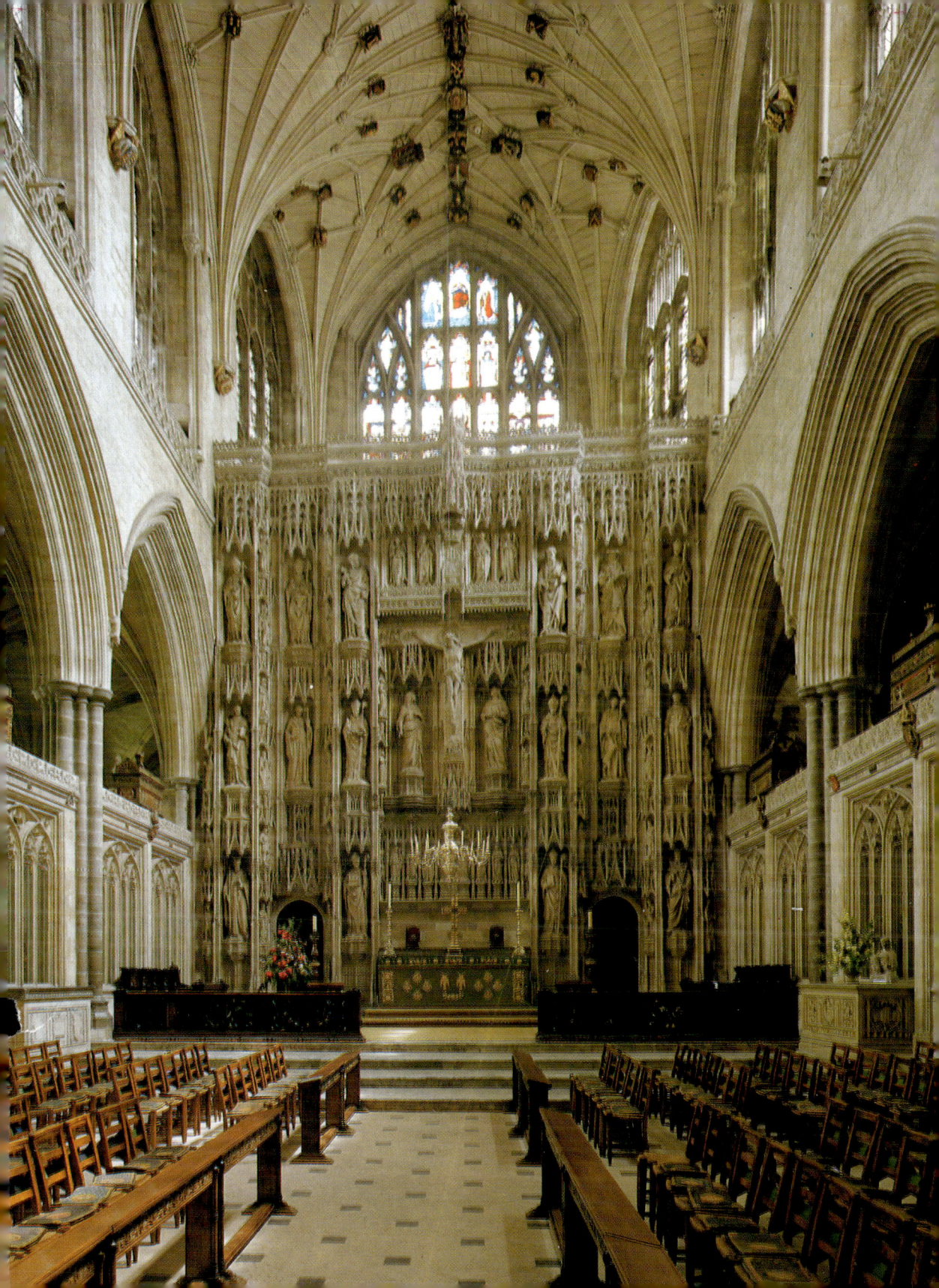

during the thrice-yearly visits of H.M. Judges of Assize. Adjoining the hall is the Crown Court building which has replaced the Assize Court.

There is some evidence that the upper parts of the High Street were damaged in the Civil War, and at Cromwell's orders Wolvesey Castle was also slighted. Yet though the city as a whole suffered little damage, the war had caused a real division in the community. In 1660 both Royalists and Parliamentarians presented petitions against each other to the House of Lords, one of the bitterest causes for contention being the way in which the Parliamentarian corporation had leased many of the city churches for secular purposes. The events of the last years of Charles II's reign had also made for local dissensions. In 1683, in the presence of the architect, Sir Christopher Wren, the foundation stone was laid of a new royal palace on the western hill. Loyal Winchester was delighted at the prospect of once more becoming a royal city; the king and his brother, the Duke of York, were both made freemen. In the last months of the reign, however, Winchester citizens

were dismayed when the king called in their charter and refused to renew it without unacceptable conditions. By controlling corporations Charles thus hoped to gain control over their Parliamentary representatives. When the king died in 1685 Winchester was still without a charter. It soon became apparent that his brother, James II, was equally determined. Despite fierce opposition, headed by Thomas Wavell, a distinguished member of that distinguished Wykehamist family, the city had to accept from James a charter nominating each and every member of the corporation and containing a large number of Roman Catholics. Yet within a few weeks James had to flee the country. One of his last actions was to return their freedom to the citizens of Winchester, in a repetition of the charter of 1587 which set out the constitution as it had emerged from the Middle Ages. This remained the governing charter of the city until the Reform Act of 1835.

The local feelings aroused by the Civil War and the struggle for the charters died down in the eighteenth century. The main political influences

were the Chandos-Buckingham families at near-by Avington House, and the Pentons of Eastgate House. When George III came to the city in 1778 he stayed with his chief loyal supporter, Henry Penton. A system had already been evolved by which the two political parties, Whigs and Tories, took it in turn to nominate the mayor and also managed the political elections. Political power was in the

Continued on page 18

★　　★　　★

ABOVE: *Kingsgate; an ancient entry into the city, and perhaps of Roman origin: above the gate is the church of St. Swithun. The gardens* (right) *planned by the late Richard Gleadowe, designer of the Stalingrad Sword, replaced houses demolished in 1919 and 1927.*

FACING PAGE: *North end of Kingsgate Street, showing* (left foreground) *the inn now called the Wykeham Arms, formerly The Fleur-de-Lis, an ancient property of the Dean and Chapter. Centre background: Kingsgate and tower of the Cathedral. The street has few outstanding buildings but its long line curving towards St. Cross is full of charm and interest.*

ABOVE: *A charming view of Great Minster Street near the Cathedral, hardly altered since the early 19th century.*

LEFT: *Jane Austen died in 1817 in this house in College Street. She had come to Winchester for medical treatment, having been ill, but continued to work here on her last great novel,* Persuasion.

FACING PAGE, above: *The northern pair of the four houses in Dome Alley built by the Dean and Chapter in 1663. In the western house (No. 7) lived Doctor Hawkins, whose father-in-law, Izaak Walton, died there in 1683. Some of the leaden rain-water pipes appear to have come from earlier Tudor buildings.*

FACING PAGE, below: *Serle's House, now the Museum of the Royal Hampshire Regiment, was built before 1748 by a famous family of wealthy Roman Catholics, the Sheldons. It seems to have been requisitioned by the Army to whom it was sold by a later owner, Peter Serle, and in the 19th century was also used as a lodging for H.M. Judges of Assize.*

16

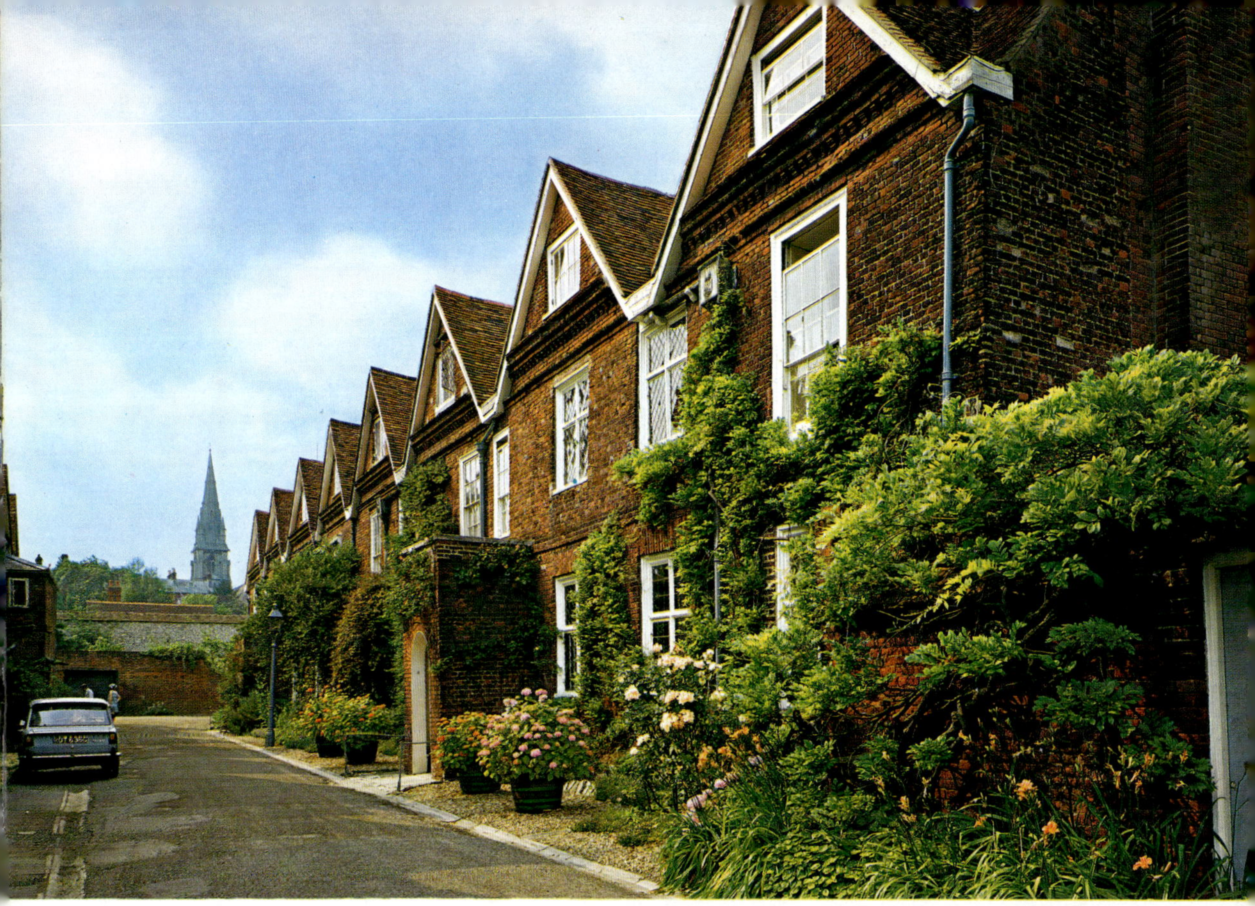

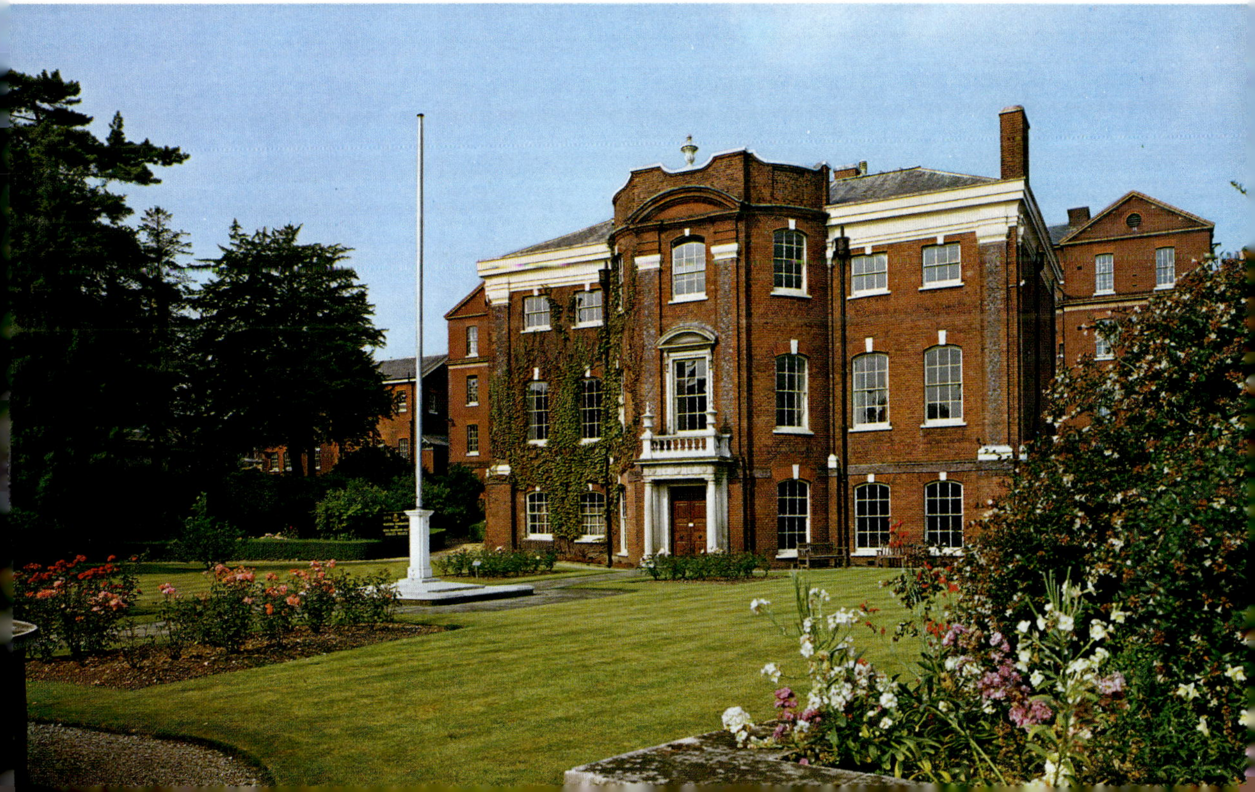

hands of a few families only. Some, like the Caves, painters and decorators, were Catholics but occasional conformers, and thus were able to hold civic office. The majority were practising Anglicans, and included men like Robert, Thomas and William Waldron, who between them held the mayoralty on twelve occasions; the Clarks, who held the town clerkship for more than half a century, and the Wavells, who were innholders at the George Inn, and two of them rectors of St. Maurice. The Rev. Richard Wavell found time to write the first really modern *History of Winchester*. There was bribery and corruption without doubt, but it is the eighteenth century which has left Winchester so much

of her present-day charm.

Work on Wren's royal palace was stopped after Queen Anne died. The unfinished building became a barracks for French prisoners, and later (1796) for English troops. It was burnt out in 1894. Though this palace was uncompleted, Winchester can still show 'Wren's' Wolvesey, the Duke of York's house (26 and 27 St. Swithun's Street) and part of the Duchess of Portmouth's residence in St. Peter Street (No. 4). The four houses which make up Dome Alley in the Close were all built in 1663. The old Market House, which stood on the corner of the Square, on the site of the present Museum, was rebuilt in 1772 at the High Street eastern junction

with Market Street. A new Winchester theatre was opened in 1785, and a replica of part of this can be seen in No. 40 Jewry Street. This theatre replaced the first floor theatre over the old market and the Assembly Rooms on the eastern corner of Upper Brook Street and the High Street. In the eighteenth century older buildings given new façades included the Queen Anne Guildhall, Colebrook House, St. John's Croft, and many of the houses in Kingsgate Street and College Street. The earliest country hospital to be founded outside London was first (1737) housed in a building in Colebrook Street (demolished 1959); a second building (1759) in Parchment Street was replaced in 1868 by the present Royal Hants County Hospital in the Romsey Road. St. John's House was redecorated in the 1790's by the local firm of Lucas, whose fine plaster decoration and panelling is much to be admired. The tradition of good building in Winchester continued into the first half of the nineteenth century, as the Corn Exchange (architect, Owen Brown Carter, 1838, with later additions by John Colson), now the Public Library, and the Market House (1857, by William Coles) bear witness. A fine façade on the western side of Jewry Street was that of the prison (built 1777, enlarged later, with a new façade by G. Money-

Continued on page 23

★ ★ ★

LEFT: *The interior of St. John in the Hospital, a chapel in the Broadway. Here the mayors of Winchester used to take their solemn oath to do right to all men during their year of office.*

FACING PAGE, above: *The War Memorial Cloister of Winchester College (architect Sir Herbert Baker) commemorates Wykehamists who died in the two world wars. Badges of the various regiments are affixed to the corbels and tie-beams of the roof.*

FACING PAGE, below: *St. John's, south. From at least 1219 the Fraternity of St. John of Winchester used to meet in St. John's House and the adjoining St. John's Chapel. It was a wealthy organisation, owning much Winchester property and using some of its income for the relief of the poor.*

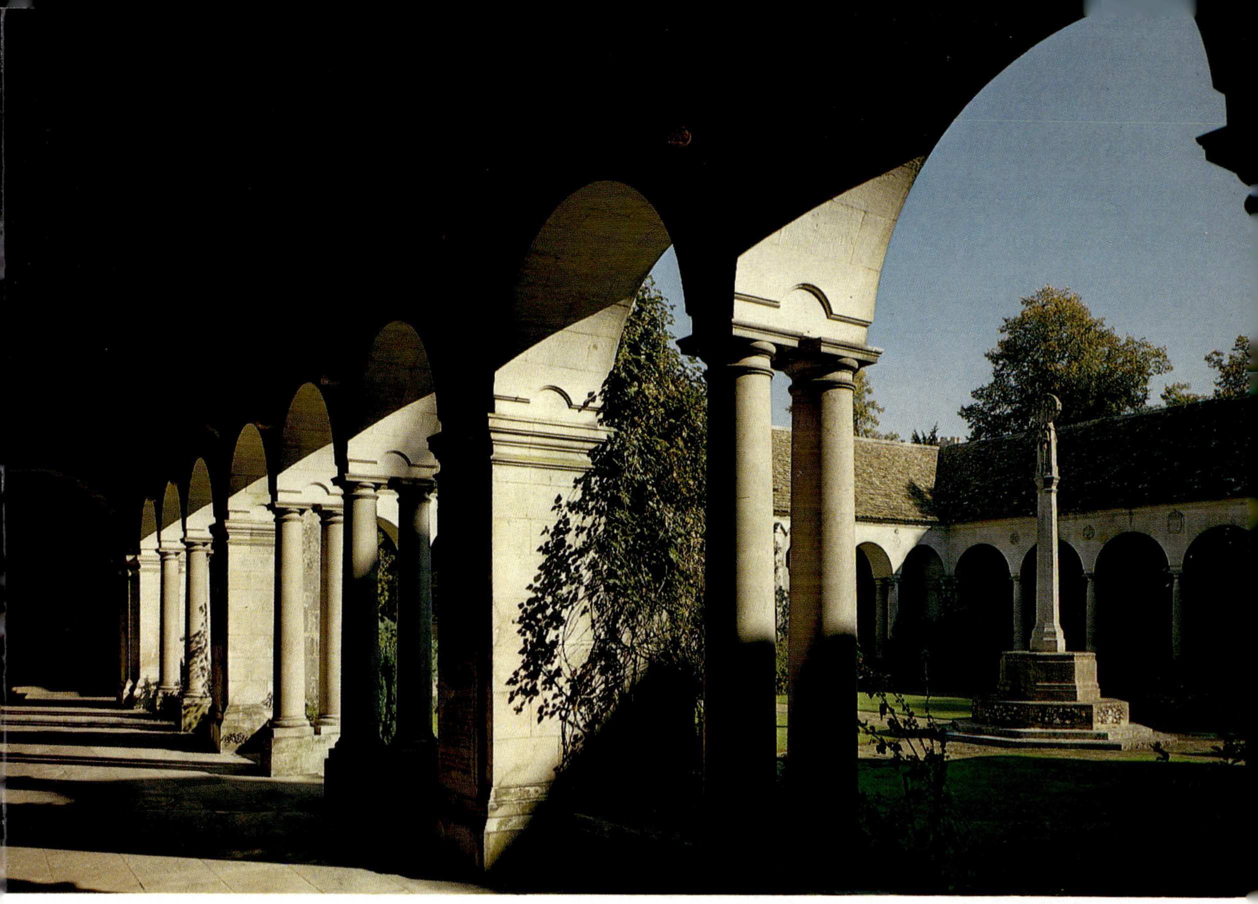

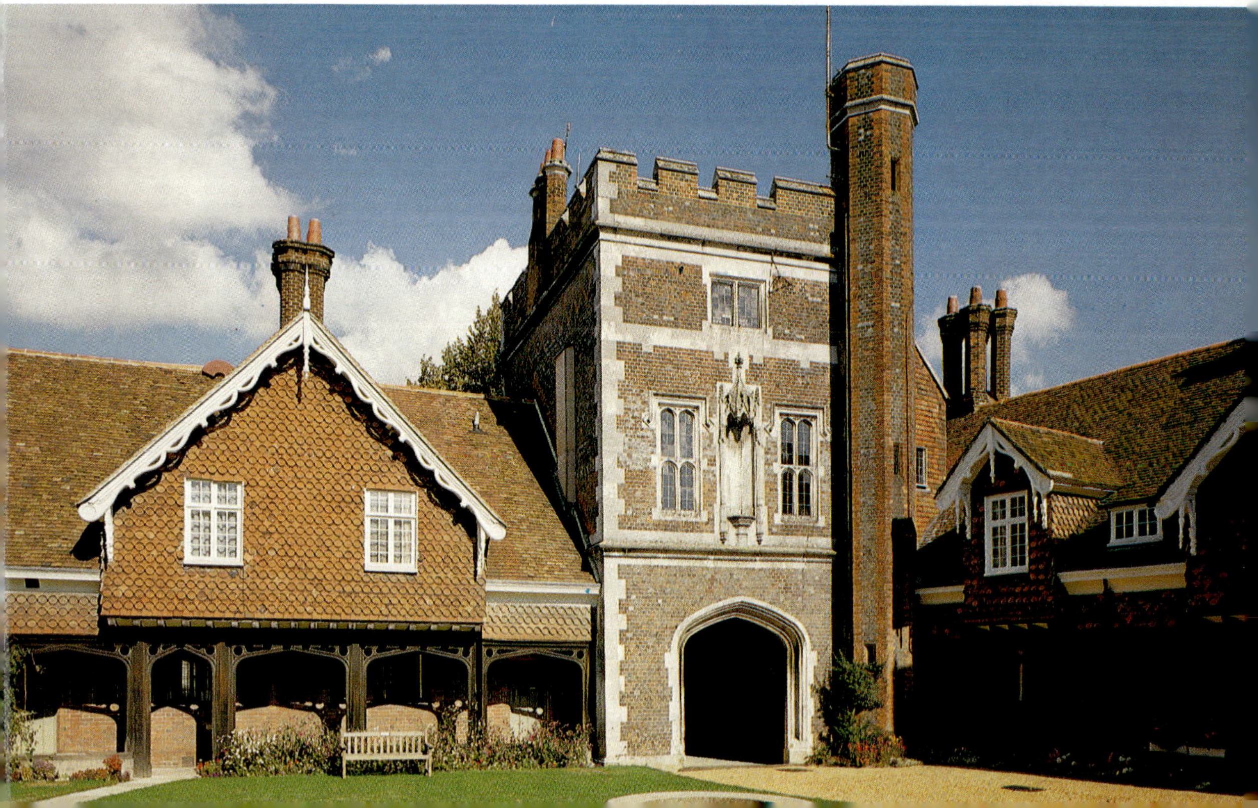

FACING PAGE: *Winchester College was founded by Bishop William of Wykeham to ensure a suitably educated and regular supply of young men for the Church. He hoped that most of his seventy scholars would go on to his earlier foundation of New College, Oxford.*

ABOVE: *Wolvesey Palace, begun in Bishop Morley's time and perhaps the work of Sir Christopher Wren, has been the home of the Bishops of Winchester since 1938 in place of Farnham Castle. Its 15th-century chapel (right) was once part of Wolvesey Castle. Many of the smaller trees and shrubs were planted by the late Archbishop Garbett, a keen gardener.*

RIGHT: *The wall of Wolvesey Castle as seen from a favourite public walk, The Weirs. The castle was erected by Henry de Blois in 1137, and slighted by Parliament after the capture of Winchester in 1645 and eventually replaced by Wolvesey Palace. The stream here is the spill-way of Wharf Mill.*

ABOVE: *Elizabeth II court. A view of the Hampshire County Council buildings, opened by H.M. The Queen in 1959. The architecture is based on a design of Mr. Cowles-Voysey, drawn up in 1936 and completed in 1959.*

LEFT: *An almshouse called Christ's Hospital was endowed in 1586 by Peter Symonds, a wealthy mercer of Winchester and Essex. Much of the stone came from Hyde Abbey. The site was previously known as Falconer's Corner. The present building has been much altered in recent years. The name of the founder is also commemorated in the local Peter Symonds VIth Form College.*

FACING PAGE: *The new Crown Court building (architect—Louis de Soissons and Partners) facing north across the Great Courtyard, with (right) the Great Hall of Winchester Castle, the scene of many famous trials including that of Sir Walter Ralegh and of Alice Lisle.*

penny). A section of its rusticated stone-work can still be seen, though the prison was sold off in lots and replaced by the present building in Romsey Road (1846–49), architect Thomas Stopher the Elder.

In the nineteenth century, too, a number of new churches were built or enlarged to meet the needs of Winchester's increasing population. St. Maurice, of Anglo-Saxon origin, was rebuilt in 1841–2 and was perhaps also Carter's work; only its much altered Norman tower now remains. Holy Trinity and Christ Church were entirely new parishes. St. Thomas, a medieval church, was rebuilt on a new site and with a spire which adds much to the Winchester landscape. There still remain many remarkable private buildings of the period, including the Pagoda in St. James' Lane (architects Hinves and Bedborough, 1849) built for a successful

blacksmith who was mayor of Southampton, and Tower House, in Tower Street, once the home of William Budden, four times mayor of Winchester, and the leader of the local Liberal party. Of the late Victorian public buildings, the Guildhall (1873) is the most striking.

An Act of 1767 'for making divers rivers navigable' applied to the Itchen, and the Itchen Canal was much used till the middle of the nineteenth century, when it was outrivalled by the railway. There are still people in Winchester today who remember getting their coal from the wharf. In 1839 the Winchester-Southampton railway was opened, and the line to London completed by 1840. A preliminary suggestion to bring the line east of the Westgate and thus through the town centre fortunately came to nought.

From about 1849 onwards the

outlying sections of the town were rapidly developed. The Pagoda in St. James' Lane was followed by the building of a number of houses in that area of Painter's Field which had once formed part of the Priory Manor of Thurmond's. At the eastern end of the town, with the decline of St. Giles' Fair, houses were built on the downs. Mildmay (or Eastgate) House was pulled down in 1844, its gardens developed as building sites, and a new road, Eastgate Street, was created.

Winchester's cathedral attracts visitors from all over the world. This brief account of the city is addressed to those who have a wish to see not only a famous jewel but also its setting. Sir Winston Churchill's great phrase springs to mind: in Winchester we may indeed see and hope to preserve 'the historic continuity of our island life'.

ABOVE: *The chapel of St. Cross Hospital, founded by 1137 by Bishop Henry de Blois for 'thirteen poor impotent men so reduced in strength as rarely or never able to raise themselves without the assistance of an-* other. *He chose the beautiful village of Sparkford, which soon became known as St. Cross. De Blois's pensioners tradition-ally wear a black gown and silver cross of Jerusalem.*

ACKNOWLEDGEMENTS: All photographs are by Sydney W. Newbery, Hon. F.I.I.P., F.R.P.S.; except those on p 8 (below) by Antony Miles; on p 13 by A. F. Kersting, F.I.I.P., F.R.P.S.; on p 12 (top) by Kenneth Scowen, F.I.I.P., F.R.P.S.; on pp 2, 3, 6, 7, 10, 11, 14, 18, 19, 22 and 23 by David Miller.

SBN 85372 050 9